Successful Living

Memorizing and Meditating

LaVonne Masters

First published in Nashville, Tennessee, by Thomas Nelson, Inc., and distributed in Canada by Lawson Falle, Ltd., Cambridge, Ontario.

Masters Publishers
Revisions 2002, 2010, 2013

Scripture quotations are from the NEW KING JAMES VERSION of the Bible. Copyright © 1979, 1980, 1982, Thomas Nelson Publishers, Inc.

ISBN: 978-1490473277

In loving memory of my beloved parents

Alfred Benjamin Tosten, DC and

Gertrude Merritt Tosten, DC

who taught me by example

to love the Scriptures.

Contents

Part One

Memorizing and Meditating

1 Living the Word

You choose; the Word empowers the choice

The flood surprised the residents of Rapid City, South Dakota when twelve to fourteen inches of rain fell in less than three hours, causing the worst and most destructive flash flood in the history of that city. The force of those raging waters that night took the lives of two hundred thirty-eight people—our three sons were among them. As our family fled our home near the flooded creek, treacherous waters ensnared our vehicle. Hour after hour, we struggled against overpowering odds to hang onto life. My husband, Ronald, myself, and our two daughters, Karen and JoAnn, were miraculously spared.

Our three sons—Stephen, twelve; Jonathan, eight; and Timothy, two-and-a-half—were gone. The pain was unbearable. We wondered if we would ever find our way out of this long dark tunnel.

Life stopped for us.

In succeeding months we learned to live one day at a time. Sometimes it was difficult to tell the days and the nights apart.

Two years passed. At first I tried adjusting to the imposed life change of loneliness without the boys by keeping busy with activities outside our home: Bible classes, shopping, eating out, anything to get away from home. When I wearied of this, I spent my energy working at home: baking, cleaning, reading, playing flute and piano. Eventually I drifted into watching endless game shows on TV. Then, one day I began to watch soap operas —with the sound turned down, you understand, so I could see how they decorated their homes, what clothes they wore, and how they styled their hair.

The next day, I turned up the sound.

What was I doing? I asked myself. Where was my life going?

There had to be a change. I had experienced the pain of sorrow long enough, and I knew I could not exist like this forever. Inside I felt as though part of me had died. My mind seemed dead. I had stopped trying. I had lost hope. I knew better than this.

In the next few months I grappled for a solution. I had to make some positive choices.

First, I decided to take responsibility for the quality of the rest of my life with positive choices. It began to dawn on mc that God could not do that for me.

Second, I chose to reprogram my thoughts. My negative thoughts, depression, and aimlessness controlled my life and resulted in dysfunctional behavior of many wasted hours in front of the Television.

I was raised in a Christian home by parents who studied and lived by the Scriptures. So, technically, I realized that the Bible had the answer for my life. I had to put this knowledge into action. So I began to fill my mind with the Word by memorizing and meditating.

The result? My life changed. The transformation soon became obvious to those around me: Instead of sorrow, depression, emptiness, and purposelessness, my life was marked by healing, peace, creativity, and purpose. Memorizing and meditating revolutionized my world so that I was able to gain perspective on all that had happened in the previous months.

I came out of my pit and felt and looked alive again.

I have continued to memorize and meditate since I lost my three sons. I have refined the program since then and have taught it to many various groups.

Not every event of my life has been perfect. However, I can tell a difference in my response to daily pressures and frustrations when I am consistently using Successful Living. Even in times when I am not consistent.

I am often reminded of the frantic pace of life we all lead when I watch the seagulls down on the waterfront in Seattle. Our family's favorite restaurant is a fish bar, where we buy fish and chips and sit outside on the pier to eat. We always share our lunch with the seagulls that float and swoop nearby.

One time when we were there, I noticed some interesting things about the gulls. The seagulls that made the most noise with their constant squawking never seemed to get much food. The ones that were quiet and determined and glided above the others had the opportunities to feed.

So it is with us when we memorize and meditate on God's Word. We become quiet and peaceful in our spirits and gain God's perspective on our circumstances so we can rise above the tensions of family demands, juggling priorities, and painful circumstances.

The effects of memorizing and meditating create a cycle: When we become quiet and peaceful in our spirits, we find time for the food of the Word of God. When we find time for the food of the Word of God, we become quiet and peaceful in our spirits.

Through memorization, we retain God's Word, and through meditation, we grasp God's Word so we can grow and mature—Successful Living: Memorizing and Meditating (M & M).

What is memorization?

Memorization is the first step in your pilgrimage into God's Word. Often people say to me, "I can't memorize anything." The fact is, however, consciousness without memory is insanity. Thus, as sane beings, we memorize what we want to, and we remember it. You may not like the idea of memorization, but don't be afraid of the word memorize. I'm not fond of it, but I use memorization as a means to an end. You can more effectively meditate when you've memorized.

Two excellent Scripture verses encouraging memorization are:

"Your word I have hidden in my heart, that I might not sin against You." Psalm 119:11

"Let not mercy and truth forsake you; bind them around your neck, write them on the tablet of your heart." Proverbs 3:3

What is meditation?

Meditation is getting to know God better, spending time with him. If you love someone, you want to be alone with that person. If you love the Lord, you want to spend time alone with Him.

When we meditate on Scripture, we fill our minds with God's Word and let the truth sink into our hearts. We allow our Father to speak to us in the depths of our souls. We commune with him and act upon instruction of his Word.

Some people are skeptical of meditation. It is Biblical. Let's look at the two Hebrew words used in the Old Testament for meditate and their meanings.

The first Hebrew word for meditate, **hagah**, appears in Joshua 1:8, "This Book of the Law shall not depart from your mouth, but you shall meditate [hagah] in it day and night, that you may observe to do according to all that is written in it. For then you will make your way prosperous, and then you will have good success."

Hagah, (pronounced haw-gaw'), means to mutter and murmur, to speak in a low inaudible voice with oneself.

The second Hebrew word for meditate, **siyach**, is in Psalm 119:15, "I will meditate [siyach] on Your precepts, and contemplate Your ways."

Siyach (pronounced see'-akh), means to ponder or muse and pray. Someone said it can be likened to a pilgrimage into God's Word.

The Random House College Dictionary defines meditate: to reflect, contemplate, a thinking over. Contemplate means to consider thoroughly; to think fully or deeply about.

The Scripture verses below illustrate the positive results of meditation. There is joy in the Lord, and finally, there is transformation by the renewing of the mind.

> "May my meditation be sweet to Him; I will be glad in the Lord." Psalm 104:34
>
> "Be transformed by the renewing of your mind that you may prove what is that good and acceptable and perfect will of God." Romans 12:2

You will enjoy the most productive, creative thoughts when you are in a quiet place: in an easy chair or maybe even lying down, completely relaxed. Start by breathing deeply. Slowly let your whole body unwind. Then think Scripture.

Meditating can be illustrated by one of my childhood experiences. I remember enjoying black walnut cake with my family when I was growing up in Iowa. However, we had to go through a process to eat that cake.

First, we went into the country and picked walnuts from the ground under those huge trees. Then when we arrived home, my sister Jeanette and I would sit out in the backyard and take the hulls off the nuts.

Next, we brought the nuts into the house to crack the shells. The best part of the process was picking the meat out of the shell. It was difficult for us to leave enough for the cake.

Later when the aroma of that luscious dessert permeated the kitchen and we tasted the masterpiece, we agreed our efforts were worth it.

One of our greatest joys as believers comes when we can share together the positive results of practicing Scriptures in our lives. However, without the efforts of M and M, this joy is unattainable.

First, we commit to choosing the verses and creating a schedule. Like picking and hulling nuts.

Second, we memorize: crack the shell of the verse. This is the first necessary energy for going below surface meaning to reach depth-meaning.

Third, we pick the meat out of the verse and eat it: We meditate on the verse, we taste the deep truths of Scripture, and savor them one at a time.

Finally, we are able to practice the Scriptures and enjoy the results: We are able to make our cake and eat it, too.

We may religiously own a Bible, but not until we read it, study it, and devour it does it become a part of us. Then we can think about those words at any time. We can live in the atmosphere of that Book anywhere. If our Bible remains unused, it is not ours. When we take the contents within, it becomes ours.

My prayer is that you will realize new growth and transformation of Successful Living as you begin to memorize and meditate on God's Word.

In part two of this book I present the five Ds of Successful Living: Memorizing and Meditating (M & M).

> Decide method
> Determine location
> Discover content
> Draw application
> Do it

In part three I discuss helpful ways for you to remain consistent for the rest of your life including how to teach kids M & M.

Part Two

Using The Five Ds

2 Decide Method

Faith comes by the Word

In my many years of practicing, then teaching, M & M, I have discovered five tried and proven options for memorizing. It may be possible that you will be able to use all of these ways at one time or another in your memorizing. Choose the option or options you feel most comfortable with, the ones that work best for you. Decide which translation works best for you and use that for all your memorization.

Try to learn all the words. Check yourself for errors. Also, try to finish what you start. This is important to your feeling of self-worth and sense of accomplishment. I don't recommend jumping around from chapter to chapter or book to book. Instead, if you start to memorize fifteen verses or a chapter or a book, stay with that section until you finish.

Option 1: Repeat the verse

Repeat. This is the most common, most reliable memorization technique with no tricks to learn. There are several important steps to help you with this approach.

Read the verse at least three times to imprint it in your mind. Block out distractions and concentrate on reading.

Space-learning. Simply learn a little now and a little throughout the day. It is another means of repetition. Every time you say a verse, repeat it three times, wait a space of time, then repeat the verse three times again, then wait a space of time. Repeat this process until you think you learned it. The spaces can be for any length of time, from one minute to several hours. Each time you say your verse after a space of time, a new imprint is made on your brain. You can say the verse three or thirty times without a break, and it will make only one impression on your mind. What makes this effective is the fact that you come back to the verses after each space of time.

Visualize. Look closely at the verse in your Bible. Notice the large words. Then close your eyes and try to see the verse in your mind's eye. Be sure to use one translation for your memorizing and meditating so you will be not become confused with different versions. It is very convenient to use electronic devices using Bible apps. Then you have your Bible wherever you go. Use the Bible translation of your choice.

Vocalize. Speaking the verse aloud and hearing it makes a double impression on the mind. This is very successful.

Write the verse three times. It is not necessary to write out every verse you memorize, but when you can't seem to memorize a verse, this gives you a breakthrough. Any activity that brings more of your senses into the learning process will help you to learn and retain information longer. Thus using the muscles in both your arm and hand to write is another reinforcement for committing verses to memory. Stretch your mind. As you repeat a verse during the day, make yourself recall much of the verse before you check yourself in the Bible.

First, try to visualize the big words of the verse in your mind, and then do the same with the small words. Experts tell us this is necessary for the development of the memory section of the brain. Relax, the words will come to you.

Option 2: Form acronyms

Use the initial letters of major words to form a word or an acrostic.

When I was memorizing Ephesians 4:31, "Let all bitterness, wrath, anger, clamor, and evil speaking be put away from you, with all malice," using this method helped me to learn it with little difficulty.

The key words of the verse are: Bitterness, Wrath, Anger, Clamor, Evil, Malice.

I took the first letter of each word, put them together, and formed the word BWACEM. Because the acronym is so odd sounding, I probably will never forget this verse.

You also can create a sentence with those letters: **B**y **W**atching **A**fter **C**hildren **E**njoy **M**ania.

Of course, you are often limited by the letters. The zanier the sentence, the longer you will remember it.

Option 3: Associate

Another way to memorize is by association. You can use either mental pictures or categories to help you with this method. When you link ridiculous mental pictures with each verse, your memory of the verse will be more permanent. Memory association experts tell us that any new information is remembered when it is associated with something already known.

This is very successful for many, and it is a procedure that may help you. If you find that you're spending more time trying to dream up the mental pictures than you are memorizing the verse, this is probably not for you.

Another way to associate is to categorize. If someone asks you to buy a list of items at the store, you can group them according to where you'll find them in the store so you can remember them more easily. For example, you may group the items according to dairy products, frozen foods, or salad ingredients.

You can apply this memory technique when you're memorizing a chapter of Scripture as well. If you were to memorize Philippians 1, you will note how many verses are included in the salutation. Then, you can note the prayer in the next verses and ask yourself the main points of the prayer. As you notice these, you can group them as follows: praise, character development, and spiritual development. Choose categories you think describe these verses.

Option 4: Record Verses

Many people enjoy recording to assist in memory work. Record the portion of Scripture you are memorizing and listen to it several times. You may choose to record one verse several times or you may want to record a whole chapter.

Another possibility is to use an audio Bible and listen to the portion of Scripture you are meditating. An excellent time to play recordings is just before you go to sleep at night. This fills your subconscious mind with the Word.

Option 5: Sing the Scriptures

When you put your verses to familiar melodies, or to melodies you create, the verses form a permanent impression in your mind.

Just as learning the ABC's to a tune inspired quicker learning when you were a child, so you'll notice you will learn your verses quicker using a tune.

The experience of singing your verses is especially uplifting when your spirits are down. The songs need not be works of art, and you need not be an excellent singer. This is a great way to enjoy yourself and learn at the same time.

As a young girl at home, one of my tasks was to wash or dry the dishes with my sister. To make the work seem lighter, we made up opera-style melodies to communicate everything we wanted to say to each other.

"Jeanette, will you wash off the table?"

"Not now, I'm scrubbing this pan."

I'm sure we made a fantastic amount of noise. I don't know how the rest of the household stood it.

In no time we were through with the dishes!

3 Determine Location

You are renewed by the Word

God gave each of us a marvelous computer for storing information: the brain. Scientists tell us the brain contains enough potential connections to receive ten new items of information per second. Everything we do every moment of our lives is controlled by its billions of components.

With this wonderful technology at our disposal, filling our minds with large portions of the Word—God's thoughts—will enable us to use these stored thoughts for our benefit in the good times and in the hard times.

Memorize sections

From experience, I recommend that you learn no less than five verses of a chapter or learn complete chapters or books rather than random verses. Most of us will admit that it is more difficult to remember verses and their location if they have been selected at random. I remember being handed two pages of verses to learn in a Sunday school class as a teenager. I memorized all the verses, but I had trouble recalling where each verse was found.

When you memorize a segment of a chapter or a book, you will be able to see in your mind's eye every verse and every chapter because of the amount of time you spend there. You can start with a few verses, a half chapter, a small chapter, or a small book. When you finish memorizing the smaller portion, you will have confidence to tackle larger portions.

Determine location

Don't let sections of Scripture scare you. Memorize each chapter or portion, one verse at a time. Learn verse one; then verses one and two; then one, two, and three. Always strive to quote the text you've learned along with each new verse you memorize.

Pray for direction

Pray for guidance to the section most beneficial for you. Simply ask God to guide you to the chapter or book you are to meditate upon.

Most people, after praying about it, do feel inclined or impressed to turn to a specific chapter or book God knows they are going to need in their lives.

I started with Philippians, then went on to Ephesians. Both books were exactly what I needed for that time in my life.

Margaret began memorizing and meditating on Psalm 91 as God directed her. Of course, she did not know what life held for her.

Three weeks later her husband died suddenly in the night of an aneurysm. She found him gasping in a chair and tried to revive him. Her efforts failed. She called her daughter for help, then the ambulance, but he was already gone. There was nothing she could have done.

The night of the funeral there was a terrible wind and rain storm. She quoted Psalm 91. It took away all fear. Before she started memorizing this psalm, she was extremely fearful. She even checked under beds to make sure no one was there.

For several months she continued quoting the words of the psalm before going to sleep at night and when she awakened in the night. Now she knew that God was going to take care of her. The comfort and healing she derived from the Scriptures could not have been obtained from any other source.

After praying about what to memorize, if you are still not certain where to begin, start memorizing a chapter that has always been your favorite or select a chapter in the area of your need. You can use the list of chapters and books on the next pages to give you some ideas. There are so many excellent Scriptures to memorize and meditate on.

You will want to meditate on the Word that will relate to your life now and the months to come for maximum effect.

Possible Scripture Choices

Half Chapters
Proverbs 31:10-31; Matthew 5:1-26; Matthew 6:1-18; John 3:1-21; Romans 8:26-39; Ephesians 5:17-33

Small Chapters
Psalm 1, Psalm 2, Psalm 23, Psalm 100, Isaiah 55

Chapters
Psalms 1, 23, 25, 37, 91, 143: God's care

Psalm 119: Love of the Word

Psalms 24, 33, 34, 126, 138, 150: Praise

Proverbs 2: Wisdom

Proverbs 31: A virtuous woman

Isaiah 40: Comfort

Isaiah 53: Redemption

Jeremiah 1: God's call

Matthew 5, 6, 7: Practical Christian living

Matthew 13: Seven parables of Christ

John 3: Born of the Spirit

John 14: Peace

John 17: Christ prays for us

Romans 4: Faith

Romans 8: Victorious living

Romans 12: Know who you are

1 Corinthians 13: Love

1 Corinthians 15: The Resurrection

Ephesians 5: Walk in love

Ephesians 6: The armor of God

Philippians 4: Positive thinking

Hebrews 11: Faith

1 John 3: Love

Small Books

Philippians, Colossians, 2 Thessalonians, 2 Timothy, Titus, Philemon, 2 Peter, 2 John, 3 John, Jude

Larger Books

Proverbs: Wisdom

John: The power of the Son of God

Romans: Doctrine and Christian duties

Ephesians: Unity of believers

Philippians: Positive thinking

1 Timothy: Counsel to a young pastor

James: Good works

1 Peter: Victory over suffering

1 John: Fellowship and love

4 Discover Content

The Word is your contact with God

We are so familiar with feeding on someone else's explanations of Scripture that we are often under the impression that only ministers and Bible teachers are qualified to discover deep truths from the Word.

Anyone who desires, may do so.

When you start feeding yourself, you'll never be completely satisfied with anything else. Nothing equals a fresh thought from God for you alone.

The first time I uncovered a truth for myself, I felt a sunburst over my spirit. This is relationship with God. God yearns for a relationship with each one of us.

In this chapter, we'll walk through the basics of meditation as we meditate on Romans 12:2. It takes a little time to develop the art of meditation. You'll soon acquire a few of your own unique techniques to use as well as some included here.

Gather resources

Before you begin to meditate, gather some materials for assistance: Bible, dictionary, index cards, journal, or an electronic device that contains all the above.

A Bible is the first book needed. Now is the time to buy a new Bible translation if you have been thinking about it. It's best to start this process with one translation so you will remember the verses and chapters you learn. Choose the translation you are most comfortable with. There are many versions of the Bible online and in Bible apps on electronic devices.

A dictionary will help in researching the definitions of words you are curious about. If you use The King James's Version you will need a Strong's Exhaustive Concordance containing glossaries of the Hebrew and Greek words in the Bible to use in researching words from Scripture.

If you desire more resource material, you can use different Bible translations, word books, and commentaries.

All of these resources are available at a local bookstore, on the internet, or available for your electronic device. The books you use are a matter of personal preference.

Two basic books to use for meditation are a Bible and a dictionary.

Record your thoughts

As you discover the content of the verses you are memorizing, you will want to make notes of definitions of words and any thoughts or applications the verses may have for your life. You can easily use a journal for this or index cards, or electronic device.

Carry your journal, cards, or device with you wherever

you go. You can record meditative thoughts whenever they occur.

A good thought's arrival cannot be predicted. Write it down immediately, and it won't be lost.

Understand the meaning

The primary way of discovering the content is to understand the meaning of the words and the verses. You don't need to research every word; only the ones you are curious about. Some verses will have no words to examine; others will have many words to study in depth.

Be aware that some of the verses you think have little to uncover may be rich in content. You may even discover deep truths in salutations.

If you use index cards write one verse per card and the number of the verse at the top left-hand corner. Write only one verse per card. In your electronic device or journal you don't need to write the verses out.

For word research I use a dictionary. For instance, in the New King James Version of the Bible, Romans 12:2 says, "Do not be conformed to this world, but be transformed by the renewing of your mind, that you may prove what is that good and acceptable and perfect will of God." I looked up the word "conformed" in the dictionary, as I was curious about this word when I memorized this verse. Definition of conformed: made similar.

From the definition in the dictionary, I began to

understand that, in the first part of this verse, Paul is warning against similarity to the world.

You can see how using the dictionary opens up new avenues of thought. The dictionary becomes indispensable in the meditation process.

If you want to study words in more depth, you can use various Bible translations, word-meaning books, and commentaries. You may want to transcribe quotations from these other sources onto your cards, your journal, and notes on your device. This is an optional step, but other references often clear up the verses you're meditating on.

If you are stumped by a verse, consciously gather all known data through the analytical processes available from many sources, and let your subconscious transform the information into useful applications. Take advantage of the hours of research done by other writers and scholars.

Ask God for understanding

In your meditation process, ask God for wisdom. Dare to ask God for practical truths to be used in your life, your business, and your relationships. In Numbers 12:8 we read of the Lord speaking openly with Moses because Moses was at home with Him. You can feel at home with God. When meditating, feel free to ask questions openly. God does not mind. That's how you grow.

As I meditated on Romans 12:2, I asked God to help

me see how I was similar to the world and how I need to be different. I asked Him to help me understand being "transformed by the renewing of your mind."

On your cards, journal, or device record the thoughts you have about each verse below the word definitions.

Consider that great thoughts are born out of seemingly insignificant thoughts, so write down everything.

Then state how you can apply this verse to your life. Once you write your thoughts and applications, you will not easily forget them, and you can refer to your writings whenever you wish to refresh your memory.

You need not write word definitions for every verse because some verses may not have any words that need to be researched. However, you can always record your meditations and applications for every verse. If you see that you haven't written anything about a verse, reread the verse and think about something to jot down.

The word meditate means to mutter and murmur. So for further enlightenment, try self-verbalization.

Pretend you are explaining your Scriptures to someone. Say them aloud. Talk to yourself. If you'd feel more comfortable with an audience, your cat or dog can be very attentive.

Children under five years old use self-verbalization to help reinforce thoughts they have that aren't fully formed. When they become older they quit because of peer pressure.

We adults can benefit by using this technique of self-verbalization in our meditations.

Paraphrase

Another aid for meditation is paraphrasing. Simply restate the verse, substituting personal pronouns, your name, and word meanings you discovered when you looked up word definitions.

For example, the paraphrase of Romans 12:2 might read: "And—your name—don't allow yourself to be made like this world, having no difference, but be changed by having your mind made new, by beginning to think differently so that you may prove or be an example of what is the good, acceptable, and perfect will of God."

You will notice that I didn't research all the words, but only the ones that were important to me; I made substitutions. Some individuals like to paraphrase every verse, because it helps them to clarify and personalize the verse, and it helps to practice the Scripture.

Remember details

As you've gone through the basics of meditation, you've been using your journal, cards, or electronic instrument to keep track of the thoughts and the applications you've made. These are some of the things you may have included:

1. Each verse with number of verse (for cards only)
2. The dictionary definition of words
3. Your thoughts and applications for each verse
4. Quotations from other sources
5. Your paraphrase

5 Draw Application

The Word is God speaking to you

Drawing the application is the most difficult to practice. Sometimes the act of application requires going against our own desires and enacting God's desires for our life. The encouraging outcome of meditation is that the longer we meditate; God's will becomes our will.

Isaiah 55:8 says, "For My thoughts are not your thoughts, nor are your ways My ways, says the Lord." We naturally do not think God's thoughts or want His ways. Yet, meditating on God's Word brings our thoughts and ways into harmony with His thoughts and ways.

In applying Scriptures to our lives, there are three important elements: use them every day, speak the verses when tempted, sense the reality of the Word.

Use the Scriptures every day

I have heard friends and well-known speakers testify how quoting one verse changed their lives. Think how much more several verses, chapters, and books will create change.

One hot July morning, in the midst of a carefree summer atmosphere, I awoke feeling grumpy at the world and everyone in it. Immediately I revealed my true feelings to my family, starting with my husband. He left for work earlier than usual that day—self preservation. Since our youngest daughter was the only human left in the house, I began to express irritation to her. She retreated to her bedroom and closed the door. Only our dog was left. When I told him I didn't like the way he made a mess when he ate, he hid from me.

As I was straightening up the kitchen, with very loud sound effects and grumblings to myself, the convicting thought entered my mind: I hadn't memorized or meditated on any new Scriptures for two weeks. I had just been repeating verses I already knew. Reluctantly, I decided to take a look at the verses I should have been working on—though I didn't want to see what they said because I was certain they would fit my life.

The first verse was Romans 6:1: "Shall we continue in sin...?" Ouch! The Scriptures didn't need to be that sharp. I knew better than to choose to be grumpy when I awakened that morning. I didn't have to continue with those attitudes or actions now. So I sat down immediately and began memorizing and meditating that verse.

It's amazing how smoothly the rest of the week went, once I began to listen to Scripture every day again.

Speak verses when tempted

There are always lessons to be learned in this life, and, occasionally, there are near-disaster experiences. I hope and pray that in all the experiences I have gone through—even the flood episode—I have learned the lessons to be learned from adversity. I don't want to live through those times again to know how to respond properly in danger and temptation. I want to learn the first time around.

Memorizing and meditating changes instincts. We can respond to hurts, storms, and temptations with trust and righteousness when we know the truth of the Scripture for our lives. Many fall away when they cannot relate the truth of the Word to their daily lives. Psalm 119:105 reassures us with, "Your word is a lamp to my feet and a light to my path."

Driving at night in the Seattle area when it's foggy and rainy is quite an adventure. Rain lashes the windshield, the road looms shadowy, and it's impossible to see where you're going. The highway department has provided raised-lane markers between lanes to help guide drivers. If you drive over these markers, you're jarred by the bumps, and you know you're driving into someone else's lane and possible destruction.

God's Word helps us as we meditate to know whether we're weaving over into the wrong lane of life. It is a light in the daytime as well as the nighttime.

When Jesus was tempted in the wilderness, as told in Matthew 4, he quoted Scripture to confront every temptation. His instinctive reaction was to use the Word against the enemy.

If you memorize and meditate, it will be easy for you to train yourself to speak the Word when you are tempted either to wrong thinking or to wrong actions.

Romans 8:31 reads, "What then shall we say to these things?" Paul didn't use "think," but "say." Declare appropriate verses aloud to situations whenever possible, as Jesus did.

For example, you might say Romans 12:2 (to yourself if others are present) when instructed by a boss to be dishonest or when friends pressure you to partake of activities you consider wrong according to Scripture. In both of these instances, Scripture will give you resolve and strength to stand firm on your convictions.

Sense the reality of the Word

As you sense the reality of the Word, the characters of the Bible will seem true-to-life. When you meditate on someone's writing; you learn a lot about the writer, get to know him or her.

For instance, when you meditate on the Gospels of John or Luke, you will come to think of the writers as your friends. Most of all, you'll become acquainted with the Lord in a new way.

At Christmastime memorize and meditate on the Christmas story, and at Easter-time the Easter story for reality during those seasons.

At night quote verses as your last thoughts before sleep and notice how the Word gives you restful sleep. Upon waking in the morning quote verses before thinking any other thoughts and experience confidence for your day.

Sense the Scriptures at work in your life. No longer will you be like the tumble weeds that bounce across the prairies. They have no root system, so they roll wherever the wind blows them. Some even become hopelessly entangled in barbed-wire fences against their own will, never to roam again.

Instead, you will be rooted and grounded in Christ.

As you use the Scriptures every day, speak verses when tried or tempted, and sense the reality of the Word, you will find yourself continuously discovering new applications.

You will experience Successful Living: M & M.

6 Do It

You are propelled by the Word

In our lives we develop habits—some good, some bad. When the alarm rings every morning, we are usually alert to its demand. When God calls us to meditation every day; how do we respond? Here are some choices to help.

Make M & M a priority

We constantly need to refine our priorities and establish habits that will help us to live faithfully by these priorities. Make Successful Living your priority.

Make a schedule

In finding priorities, the first thing to select is a time for M & M. This will be different for everyone. If you leap out of bed in the morning singing, morning may be your best time. If you move slowly in the morning, you'll do your most creative meditating around the middle of the day or in the evening.

Some suggestions for M & M time are first thing in the morning, during break times at work, during your lunch hour, immediately after work, in the early evening, or just before going to bed. Choose a specified period for memorization and meditation every day whenever possible.

Take a few minutes every month to plan priorities. Fit your life around M & M instead of trying to fit M & M into your life.

It has been discovered that singles and childless couples have about forty hours of leisure, dual-career couples or parents have about twenty hours of leisure, and senior citizens have over forty hours of leisure every week.

We fill this free time with many temporary activities without lasting results: the lawn needs mowing, the groceries need buying, and the mountains are invariably calling to us for exploration. But the benefits of meditation will last for eternity.

Use Successful Living as your study and devotional time. Choosing M & M will give you a consistency that will thrill you as you realize every day you are building more of the Scriptures into your life. You never need to be in uncertainty about where to study or how to have devotions.

As it's not possible to study the whole Bible at one time, and you can M & M in only one place at a time, it doesn't matter whether you're not reading and studying in other parts of the Bible. The key is to concentrate on one portion of Scripture at a time.

Put Forth the Effort. What you put into memorizing and meditating is what you get out of it. The Bible teaches about the principle of giving and receiving in Mark 4.

Whatever measure is given out will be the measure that will return again.

Diligent and consistent effort yields results. If you continue faithfully in meditation, you'll be amazed in the long run at the subtle and gradual changes that have taken place in your heart, mind, and life.

Set goals

Another important step in establishing your priorities is deciding each week how many verses you will be able to learn. Be realistic about your goals. It's important for your self-esteem that you achieve the goals you have set. You may have a fairly open week and can spend time on five verses. Your next week might be much busier, so you'll only be able to allow time for one verse. If your schedule becomes more hectic than you anticipated and you are unable to reach your goal, don't be discouraged. Just pick up the verses the next week.

You are not competing with anyone. Only you will be able to determine your pace for memorizing and meditating.

If you take a trip by car from Boston to Seattle on Interstate 90, it is a trip of 3,000 miles. It seems overwhelming when you look at the whole, but when you break it down from city to city, it becomes attainable.

This 3,000-mile trip can be likened to a book or chapter you choose to M & M. The cities along the way are your weekly goals. Just as you drive one mile at a time, so also you learn one phrase or one verse at a time. Before you know it, you arrive at the destination.

Following is a suggested weekly guide you can use for M & M. The first day of your week can start on any day of the week.

For example, you can start with Wednesday as your first day and continue with the fourth and fifth day on the weekend with Monday and Tuesday as your sixth and seventh days.

You might also memorize all your verses the first day and review and research the rest of the days. Some people like to look up all their words on the first day and concentrate on memory and application on the rest of the days.

Vary this guide for your schedule, but be sure to have a regular memorization and meditation time five days a week. For as little as five to fifteen minutes a day, five days a week, Successful Living will be yours.

Suggested Weekly Guide

First Day: 5 to l5 minutes

1. Write out two to five verses. (For cards only)
2. Start with prayer.
3. Memorize first verse.
4. Research words you are curious about.
5. Write personal application.

Second Day: 5 to l5 minutes

1. Start with prayer.
2. Memorize second verse.
3. Research unknown words.
4. Write personal application.

Third Day: 5 to 15 minutes

1. Start with prayer.
2. Review verses or memorize third verse.
3. Additional research if desired.
4. Write personal application.

Fourth Day: 5 to 15 minutes

1. Start with prayer.
2. Review verses or memorize fourth verse.
3. Additional research or research unknown words.
4. Write personal application.

Fifth Day: 5 to 15 minutes

1. Start with prayer.
2. Review verses or memorize fifth verse.
3. Additional research or research unknown words.
4. Write personal application.

Sixth Day: Quote all verses in current selection.

Seventh Day: Quote all verses in current selection.

Pray

Sometimes our meditation hits us like a bolt of lightning. Other times the process seems dull—maybe too practical. Here are some things to sustain you: Spend time in prayer along with meditation, clear your mind before meditation, rely on the Holy Spirit to teach, and trust that the Word is doing its work.

Try to begin each M & M session with prayer. Prayer is effective in any posture, lying, sitting, or kneeling. Start with prayer wherever you are. Before you know it, prayer and meditation will mesh together as one.

Empty mind of cares and fill with the Word

Cut through the clutter. By an act of the will, as you throw problems out of your mind, you will open yourself to exciting truths with more creativity in every area of your life.

Learn of the Holy Spirit. John 14:26 says, "But the Helper, the Holy Spirit will teach you all things, and bring to your remembrance all things that I said to you." The Holy Spirit will open up the Scriptures to you and will bring verses to memory, even verses you learned years ago, and meditative thoughts to mind when they are needed for living, teaching, or counseling.

Trust in the quickening power of God's Word. Listen for the Scriptures you are memorizing and meditating in sermons and in Bible studies. You will begin to see new applications of the Scriptures for your life. The Word will be alive for you, and you will become alive through the Word. God merely spoke the Word, and all creation came into being. As Romans 4:17 states, "God, who gives life to the dead, and calls those things which do not exist as though they did."

He can take nothing and make it into something. God gives life to our hearts, souls, and minds.

It is Christ who gives us life, power, and strength to work out our goals to overcome distressing pressure that comes from without and within. In his words are spirit and life—Successful Living, M & M.

Relax

Many cultures around the world have "siesta" or rest time every day for a few hours in the afternoon. When you're not used to this, you may feel uncomfortable taking a few moments in the beginning, middle, or end of the day for meditation, and you'll catch yourself dwelling on all the things you need to do.

Stay with it. This special quiet time is for your strength, so there's no need to feel uptight about taking the time to memorize and meditate. Consciously choose relaxation.

Free yourself of stress to improve memory

Stress can be a problem, and stress management can

be the root of physical, emotional, and spiritual health. A small amount of stress gives us a sense of mental alertness, high motivation, and improved memory. However, when too stressed, we experience an overload, which causes fatigue, irritability, diminished memory, and maybe even illness.

Occasionally, we bring undue strain on ourselves by trying to measure up to expectations others may have for us that aren't in tune with our gifts or temperament.

Meditation will relieve the stress we experience in our daily lives, such as tension from our jobs or families or relationships. Start by imagining yourself in meditation, and soon it will be a reality.

Start an exercise program

Regular exercise relieves stress, makes you feel alive, and sharpens the mind. I'm not advocating that you become an exercise fanatic. Everyone can be involved in some form of exercise like walking, swimming, or bicycling for as little as ten minutes a day.

Doctors tell us that physical exertion increases the flow of blood to the brain and increases mental powers. Thus, not only will you feel the difference in your body; but you'll see the evidence in your meditations as well.

Think positively

Say, "I Can." When you say you can't, you can't, and

you immediately set up a mental block for any new learning. Some people tell me they can't memorize. Then just do what you can. If you can't memorize, concentrate on meditation only.

Researchers have discovered that negative attitudes also cause "the blues," that distort memory and perspective. Negative people see bad in everything. To M & M we need one of the basic skills of survival—positive thinking.

I once heard a story about a negative person who threw away his alphabet cereal one morning because he saw a dirty word in it.

Then there was the young man who lost his job in advertising because he didn't have anything good to say about the product.

Of course, both those stories are ridiculous

The point to us all is: Be positive and enjoy the benefits!

Part Three

Making It Work

7 Partner

You are upheld by the Word

When I tried to memorize and meditate without a partner, it didn't work very well. Most of us need a partner for consistency.

The ideal partner is an acquaintance. Intimate friends or family members are not always best because of your familiarity with them. However, they cannot be ruled out. This varies with everyone's social structures.

When we moved to a different city, I didn't have a partner the first month we were there. One day I became desperate and told the Lord I couldn't live another day without a partner. That night Norma, one of the women of our church, asked me to share with her what I had learned about memorizing and meditating. God had been speaking to her about being in his Word in a deeper way. God answers prayer; doesn't He?

The following guidelines make partnership successful.

Call once a week

Call your partner every week at a pre-appointed time to listen to each other's verses. I can't emphasize enough the importance of this step. This makes the whole program effective.

Ask the Lord to help you find a time convenient for

both of you. I called my partner every Saturday morning between nine and ten A.M. This worked out great for us.

You and your partner can take turns initiating the call, or one of you can make the call every week. You may, instead of making a telephone call, want to meet a few minutes before or after a church meeting, if you attend the same church, or meet for breakfast, lunch, or coffee once a week. Do what works best.

Keep your call brief

During this call, say your current verses for your partner. Unless you have an agreement to say all the verses of your chapter or section, it is not necessary to say all the verses every week; just quote new memory work. Then you can make some brief comments you think might be a blessing to your partner concerning some of your meditative thoughts. Be careful of using this time for unloading problems on your partner. This can destroy the uplift of the Scriptures.

Indicate corrections

Have your Bible ready to check your partner as he or she says the verses. When your partner is finished, tell him or her in an encouraging way of changes that need to be made. Be careful of being excessively picky. Then, have your partner correct you when you have finished saying your verses.

Be faithful

Faithfulness will benefit you and your partner. Try not to make excuses to your partner when she or he calls unless you have an emergency. Putting your partner off is not being fair to either of you. If you have made a commitment, follow through.

Pray, inspire, encourage

Of course, you will, at times, struggle with this commitment. You need each other's prayers, inspiration, and encouragement through the good times as well as the discouraging times. Consider this: You are helping each other build for eternity. It is worth the time and the effort.

Start M & M Club

Women, men, youth, children, couples, friends, neighbors, a social group, or a church class are some of the people groups that work well to form an M & M Club.

The club can be highly organized or not; either type can work well. You decide.

Meetings can be in a home, at a church, in a public place, or local coffee shop. Wherever it's convenient for all members to convene.

Choose a leader that is voted into office or approved of by consensus or form a committee that decides on policy and location and time of meetings.

Meetings can be weekly, biweekly, monthly, or bimonthly. By agreement or voting decide what fits everyone's schedule.

The length of the meeting can be for an hour or two hours. Choose the length before hand so everyone can schedule this time into their calendars.

Guidelines for meetings

Find partners. Choose partners within the group by drawing names or a method the group decides upon. They can say their verses together at every meeting.

Share meditations. Avoid allowing one person to monopolize a meeting. Determine to give time to anyone desiring to share thoughts.

Avoid doctrinal arguments. When each one that desires, tells what his or her Scripture meditation means personally, there need be no argument.

Focus on M & M. Before or after the meeting, of course, there is time for other social conversations.

Pray and encourage. Take a moment at every meeting to pray for one another. Determine to make these times positive, a spiritual uplift.

8 Review

You are sustained by the Word

The Word will remain in the memory forever. However, review keeps the verses fresh. Here are some helpful hints for every chapter:

Record in your Bible or electronic device the date you start and the date you finish memorizing a chapter. This will be of interest to you as you continue to memorize and meditate.

Enter in your Bible or device a one or two-word caption summarizing each chapter. It may be a word no one else would choose for that chapter, but it needs to be a key thought that will trigger your memory about the entire content of the chapter. Sometimes it is necessary to break down the chapter because of a drastic shift in subject matter, so perhaps use another word caption halfway through the chapter. Examples of one-word captions for the first few chapters of Romans are: Chapter 1-Sin, Chapter 2-Law, Chapter 3-Justification.

Underline or highlight verses that have special significance to you. We know the importance of underlining and highlighting verses so we can find them quickly. This also helps to imprint the verse in our minds.

Review word for word, once a week, the previous chapter you learned when you start a new chapter; repeat this for three consecutive weeks, then discontinue. For instance, if you finished memorizing the first chapter of Philippians, as you start with the first few verses of chapter two, review your first chapter at least once, word for word, recalling your meditative thoughts. For the next two weeks, you will quote chapter one again, as you continue to memorize chapter two. After your third week of review, you do not need to recite the first chapter anymore unless you desire.

9 Enjoy Benefits

You are recreated by the Word

If someone offered to give you a map to help you find buried treasure, would you accept it? Of course you would. You would quickly make plans to find that treasure and benefit from it.

Treasures are available from the Word of God, by the map of Successful Living: M & M. They are: increased intelligence, improved health, stimulated creativity, relief from stress, attained potential, consistent devotions, and eternal treasure.

Increased intelligence

When you seek God's wisdom first, increased intelligence can follow. Students who M & M consistently often testify that their grades improve from Cs and Bs to As.

You gain not only wisdom, but also love, stability, and righteousness. The attributes of God will be demonstrated in your life as well.

Improved health

It is an established fact that avoidance of disease starts in the mind. What you think can make you well or sick.

You will enjoy improved health as you allow

Scriptures to govern your thoughts, and you will no longer be controlled by impure motives and emotions or harmful anxieties but rather positive thoughts of success.

Stimulated creativity

Have you truly discovered God's plan for you? Your niche? Have you recognized the purpose that is entirely in tune with your gifts and your inner self? Do you have a sense of completeness?

Spend some time with God every day in M & M, communing with him and thinking His thoughts, and you will be surprised at the results. God's creativity will abound in your life, beyond what you dared hope for.

Stress relief

Acquire faith and peace for every day and reserve for emergencies. A wise person has said, "Sometimes God calms the storms, and sometimes he calms his child during the storm." You will have the peace to endure whatever comes your way.

I experienced a "storm" firsthand one beautiful spring afternoon in the Black Hills. Seated in a comfortable recliner, meditating on Ephesians 3:16, "That He would grant you, according to the riches of His glory, to be strengthened with might through His Spirit in the inner man," and drinking from the mountain scene that stretched out before me through the picture windows of our living room, my spirit revived.

The grandfather clock chimed. *JoAnn needs to be picked up from school. If I hurry I won't be too late*, I thought.

I bounced out of the chair, picked up my handbag and car keys, tore down the stairs to the garage, got into the car, put the key in the ignition, started the car, gazed into the rearview mirror, and backed out *through* the garage door.

I was shattered. So was the door.

Karen, who was in her room, ran downstairs and gawked with disbelief, "What happened?"

"I don't want to talk about it," I said through clenched teeth as we both started to pick up the pieces of glass for the garbage can and stack the wood for the fireplace.

As my sanity gradually returned, I sent Karen off to school to pick up JoAnn and went upstairs to call my husband at his office to prepare him for what he would face when he came home.

Unbelievably; I reached him right away. "Honey, you'll never guess what happened." I started to cry—crying always helps a little. "I thought this only happened to people in books, but," sniff, sniff, "I backed out through the garage door."

A long pause, then...laughter.

I had prepared myself for everything but that. How could he laugh at a time like this?

After our conversation, I slinked to the garage to cover my handiwork before the neighbors could see. I put up the remains of the door to hide it, and as I did, more glass and wood fell. The girls were now home and helped me collect all the bits.

Just then, our church elder's wife drove by; "Aren't you going to wave to her, Mom?" JoAnn asked.

"No! Don't move. She may not see us."

Stress—this was stress. All I longed for right then was for the last half hour of my life to be bleeped from my life.

It took a few days for me to recover. But I had a reserve for the days following this "emergency." When the verse I had been meditating on began to take effect, I sensed a strengthening inside. Strength for the day. Strength to laugh about it in the future.

Attained potential

You will reach your potential not when you are dependent upon people, talents, and environment, but when you place your confidence in Christ for that capacity. Philippians 1:6 tells us: "Being confident of this very thing, that He who has begun a good work in you will complete it." God will complete you when you avail yourself of His Word for development. With this confidence, you can face and overcome the obstacles to reach your potential.

Consistent devotions

Memorizing and meditating is a solution for a consistent, devotional time with the Lord. It is a consistent way to commune with God, feed on his Word, and find answers to life's problems.

The only creature I know of who has not benefited from feeding on the Word was our dog Skippy. He ate the entire book of Philippians out of my Bible.

Instead of his disposition improving, he got mean.

We had to get rid of him.

Eternal treasure

A story is told of a long-ago Persian, Ali Hafed, who lived not far from the River Indus. He owned a very large farm with gardens, vineyards and grain fields. He was very wealthy and content—until he heard about diamonds.

Then he became discontent. Ali Hafed wanted, indeed craved, a diamond mine and what it could buy him.

So he sold his farm, collected his money, left his family with a neighbor, and went in search of a diamond mine. He wandered the world searching. Searching. Until all his money was spent and he was in rags, poverty, and wretchedness.

Finally, in despair, he cast himself into the sea.

The man who bought Ali Hafed's farm led his camel into the garden to drink one day. As the camel put its nose into the shallow water, Ali Hafed's successor noticed a curious flash of light from the white sands of the stream.

A huge diamond.

Soon, a whole diamond mine was discovered, the Golcanda mine, which produced the largest jewels on earth.

If only Ali Hafed had known about the diamond mine. If only he had found the treasure right in his own backyard.

In your home there is treasure: the Bible. With a little patience, you will find the benefits for your life. You need not search the world. It is in your Bible.

It's M & M.

10 Teach Kids M & M

The best way to guide children spiritually is to help them learn the teachings and principles of the Bible through memorizing and meditating. Teach them to judge everything by Scripture, so they will realize that all other ground is inconsistent.

There are fifty-two weeks in a year, and a child attends school from kindergarten through twelfth grade, thirteen years. If a child learns just one verse of Scripture a week for thirteen years, he or she will have learned 676 verses before he or she graduates from high school. Here are some possibilities:

The book of Mark, 678 verses or

Several selections:
Sermon on Mount: 111 verses
Ephesians: 155 verses
Philippians: 104 verses
1 Timothy: 113 verses
James: 108 verses
1 John: 105 verses
Total verses: 696

Planting this amount of Scripture into your children's minds and hearts will help them to develop positive actions and attitudes. You will, indeed, be "training up your child."

Before you begin

Choose a Bible translation your child can appreciate and understand. It's important that your child use one Bible translation throughout his or her years of memorizing and meditating. So start with a translation the child won't outgrow.

As with the adults Successful Living, children may use an index card system, a journal or an electronic device. Each of your children need their own device or cards for his or her memory work.

Have your child write one verse per card, if he or she uses cards, and record any word meanings you and your child discover. Let your child write or record any thoughts or applications for each verse in the journal or electronic device used for M & M.

Be sensitive to your child's learning capacity and select only the number of verses you think he or she can comfortably handle each week.

One grandmother told me that her son and his wife didn't seem to have time to start her granddaughter with M & M, so she has started teaching her grandchild. The grandfather printed out the verses on the cards, and both grandparents became involved in teaching Scriptures to their granddaughter.

What a great way to establish bonds with grandchildren!

If you use cards, keep the cards of the current verses visible by placing them on the refrigerator with magnets or tacking them to the child's bulletin board. Assemble a box for each child to store their cards in.

When each child has finished memorizing and meditating each verse. Record the date the work was completed on the cards or in the journal or electronic device.

Decide method

Have your child choose from the five suggested options for memorizing. The one he or she is comfortable with.

Option 1: Repetition. Memorizing is easy for kids. Their minds are fresh and quick. The most common way children learn information and facts is by repetition. Be sure they say the verse aloud three times, visualize the verse, and write the verse three times.

Option 2: Form acronyms. This is particularly effective to use for verses that list several things.

Option 3: Association. If your child does not respond to repetition, teach association, relating each verse to a picture you or your child draws to depict each verse. Be sure to keep the picture simple.

Option 4: Record verses. Record portions of Scripture so they can listen throughout the day. If they play the Scriptures just before going to sleep at night, they'll sleep better and perhaps learn the verses more easily.

Option 5: Sing Scripture. Encourage children who enjoy singing to make up songs using the words of verses that are special to them.

Determine location

Ask the Lord to guide you to the portion of Scripture each of your children needs. It is less work for you if all your children are working on the same Scriptures at the same time. However, there are times when one child may need a different Scripture because of his or her specific needs for encouragement or instruction or because he or she is not at the same level as the other children. For age-appropriate Scripture references refer to the end of this chapter.

Discover content

Research key words in the dictionary and, if your child can write, have the child write the definitions on index cards. You may not want to use a dictionary with preschoolers. Instead, use examples to teach word meanings. To teach the meaning of the word kind, you might demonstrate politeness. When a sibling takes advantage of the younger child, show him or her how to be kind in return. Use a dictionary along with active experience to teach word meanings to children aged six to twelve. A teen can look up words by themselves to discover word meanings.

Simplify thoughts and explanations for each age level. Take an active part in sharing and discussing the verses with your children so they may learn to meditate on their own intellectual levels. Insert the child's name in appropriate verses to personalize the verses.

Keep it simple.

Draw application

Prompt creative thinking by asking questions, such as: What do you think about this verse? What do you feel about this verse? How can this verse fit into or apply to your life? Open-ended questions, such as these, affirm your child's ideas and inspire creative thinking.

This is a good time for you as a parent to add new ideas into the discussion with your child.

Guide each child in relating each verse to life experiences. Use every opportunity during the week to point out, in a casual manner, how the verses your child is learning relates to her or his life.

Ask God to help you be alert to living object lessons and trust that the Holy Spirit will enlighten your child's mind to the truth of the Word for applications to life. The

Holy Spirit speaks and makes Scripture real to a child, too.

Remember that in order for your children to understand Scriptures, not only must they feel and experience Scripture for themselves, but also they need to see your example.

Otherwise, they will develop a confused picture of what the Bible means.

Incorporate applications into your prayer time with each child. This aids the child in applying instruction of the Scriptures immediately. For example, if your child learns the verse, "Be kind," he or she can ask God to help him or her be kind to brothers and sisters and friends. Specific prayer affects specific response.

Do it

Schedule M & M times with your children. Choose the time that fits best with everyone's schedules. Work on memorization in the morning and meditation during the day and in the evening. Ideas for times: whenever you are doing something together, mealtimes, or family times when there can be interaction with you and other family members with questions and discussions.

Pray for the Lord's help. Ask the Lord to help you as a parent to guide and instruct your children. Use part of M & M time for prayer, especially in the evening. Many parents say prayers with their children before they go to sleep, so using this time will be familiar to both of you.

Many children have trouble sleeping and experience nightmares. M & M will bring peace to them as nothing else will.

Relax with your children. Lie down on the bed or curl up in a chair with them. For this to be successful, there has to be a relaxed atmosphere. Children respond and learn more quickly when "it's fun." Avoid pressuring them. Use this time to get to know them better and to guide them into knowing God.

Be positive about M & M. Encourage your children in their progress. Sometimes children will make mistakes when saying their verses for you. When this happens, repeat the verse in the correct form without drawing attention to the error. You will be modeling the correct version in a positive manner that encourages discussion and does not dampen their desire.

If your children are struggling with the program, find a different method for memorizing or a unique way of meditating. Always keep your comments positive.

Early childhood specialists say that positive comments from significant adults provide important guideposts for children's behavior. Focus on improvement and avoid comparisons or competition.

These guidelines are necessary for an enthusiastic response from your children. Children will always associate the emotions they had during M & M with the Word of God. So make these moments cheerful and pleasant.

Extra helps

Use a five day schedule. On the weekend, give M & M a rest unless an opportune moment occurs for casually teaching the meaning or application of a verse your child is working on.

Incentives are effective aids. Incentives are not bribery. Receiving rewards for behavior reassures your child that the content of the verses they are learning merit value at home. As long as rewards are necessary, feel comfortable about using them to reinforce your values to your child.

Make the rewards appropriate for the amount of verses learned and for your child's age: a piece of candy for one verse, a picnic for a month of verses, a shopping trip for six months of verses, and so on. Below are a few incentive suggestions arranged by age group. (Add some of your own ideas for incentives, also.)

Ages 2 to 5

A sticker, ice cream, first Bible, a picnic, stay up later, shopping trip with Mom or Dad, candy, inexpensive toy, money, help Mom bake cookies, new book, trip to the zoo or water park

Ages 6 to 12

New book, new clothing item, toy model, money, attend a sporting event with parents, permission to go to a friend's house, special bike ride, slumber party at home, lunch at a restaurant, electronic device, favorite game

Ages 13 to 18

New "fad" item, invite a friend to stay overnight, gift card, family car for one day, item for collection, money, privilege to stay up late one night (at home!), electronic gadget

If I polled parents who read this book, I'm sure the response will be that you want the best for your children.

We teach our children habits for good health and cleanliness. We send them to school to learn. Any extracurricular activity they desire, and we can afford, is theirs: music, sports, hobbies, travel, electronics.

However, I have heard parents say, "I'm not going to force my children to attend church or make them read the Bible. I don't want to make them rebellious."

When children are encouraged to do so with the right spirit, they rarely become rebellious about going to church or learning the Word. It is the child who does not learn faithfulness in church attendance and a love for the Scriptures who has no foundation of values and will, in the end, becomes rebellious.

The truth is if you live the way you expect your children to live, they will not depart from your spiritual training and will grow up to respect and revere you and the God you serve.

M & M for Kids

Ages 2 TO 5

First rainbow: Genesis 9:8-17

Ten Commands: Exodus 20: 1-17

Greatest command: Deuteronomy 6:1-9

Choosing good: Joshua 24:14-18

God's call: 1 Samuel 3:1-10

Good and the bad: Psalm 1

Shepherd Psalm: Psalm 23

Praising God: Psalms 100; 150

God's help: Psalm 121

Giving to God: Malachi 3:8-12

Beatitudes: Matthew 5:1-12

Lord's Prayer: Matthew 6:9-13

Birth of Christ: Luke 2:1-20

Resurrection: Luke 24:1-12

New Birth: Romans 10:9-10, Ephesians 2:8-9

Spirit living: Galatians 5:22-26

Forgiving others: Ephesians 4:25-32

Armor of God: Ephesians 6:10-20

Right Thinking: Philippians 4:4-9

Ages 6 TO 12

History of creation: Genesis1-2

First rainbow: Genesis 9:8-17

God's call: Genesis 12:1-4; Ex. 3:1-10; 1 Samuel 3:1-10

Ten Commands: Exodus 20:1-17; Matthew 22:36-40

Greatest command: Deuteronomy 6:1-9

Good over evil: Deuteronomy 30:11-20; Joshua 24: 14-18

Encouragement: Deuteronomy 31:6-8; Isaiah 41:8-13

Success: Joshua 1:7-9; Psalm 1

Obedience: 1 Samuel 15:22-23; Matthew 7:21-23

Good and the bad. Psalm 1

Who Is God? Psalm 19

Shepherd Psalm: Psalm 23

Trust God: Psalm 37:3-8; 118:5-9; Proverbs 3:3-6

Security in God: Psalm 46

Praising God: Psalms 100; 150

Word of God: Psalm 119:1-16, 33-48

God's help: Psalm 121

Sow and reap: Ps. 126:4-6; Luke 8:4-18; Galatians 6:6-10

Peace: Isaiah 26:1-4; 55:11-13; Philippians 4:4-9

Daniel's obedience to God: Daniel 1:6-21

Giving to God: Malachi 3:8-12; Matthew 6:1-4

Disciples: Matthew 4:18-22; Mark 3:13-19; Luke 5:1-11

Beatitudes: Matthew 5:1-12

Lord's Prayer: Matthew 6:9-13

Talents: Matthew 25:14-30

Good Samaritan: Luke 10:30-37

Forgive others: Luke 17:1-4; Ephesians 4:25-32

Birth of Jesus: Luke 2:1-20

Resurrection: Luke 24:1-12

Miracle of Jesus: John 6:1-21

Free from sin: Romans 8:1-11

New Birth: Romans 10:9-10; Ephesians 2:8-9

Love: 1 Corinthians 13

Spirit living: Galatians 5:22-26

Armor of God: Ephesians 6: 10-20

Right thinking: Philippians 4:4-9

Fellowship with God: 1 John 1

Ages 13 TO 18

History of creation: Genesis 1-2

The Fall of man: Genesis 3

First rainbow: Genesis 9:8-17

God's Call: Genesis 12:1-4; 1 Samuel 3:1-10

Ten Commands: Exodus 20:1-17; Matthew 22:36-40

Greatest Command: Deuteronomy 6:1-9

Good over Evil: Deuteronomy 30:11-20

Encouragement: Isaiah 41:8-13; Matthew 14:22-32

Success: Joshua 1:7-9; Psalm 1

The walls of Jericho: Joshua 6

Obedience: 1 Samuel 15:22-23; Matthew 7:21-23

Good and the bad: Psalm 1

Who Is God? Psalm 19

Shepherd Psalm: Psalm 23

King and His Kingdom: Psalm 24

Help for hard times: Psalm 25

Trusting God: Psalm 34; 37:3-8; Proverbs 3:3-6

Security in God: Psalm 46

Love for God's House: Psalm 84

Safety with God: Psalm 91

Praising God: Psalms 100; 150

Word of God: Psalm 119:1-6, 33-48

God's help: Psalm 121

Sow and reap: Luke 8:4-18; Galatians 6:6-10

God made me; Psalm 139

Wisdom for youth: Proverbs 3

Value of diligence: Ecclesiastics 11

Peace: Isaiah 26:1-4; 55:11-13

Power of God: Isaiah 40:9-13

Promises of Christ: Isaiah 55

Daniel's Obedience: Daniel 1:6-21

Giving: Malachi 3:8-12; Matthew 6:1-4; 2

Called Disciples: Matthew 4:18-22; Mark 3:13-19

Sermon on the Mount: Matthew 5-7

Lord's Prayer: Matthew 6:9-13; John 17

Parables: Tares, Sower: Matthew 13:24-30; Luke 8:4-18

Parables: Treasure, Pearl: Matthew 13:44; 13:45-46

Parables: Matthew 25:14-30; Luke 10:30-37

Jesus miracles: Mark 5:21-43; Luke 5:17-25; John 2:1-12

Discipleship: Mark 8:34-38; Luke 14:26-33; John 8:31-36

Prayer of faith: Mark 11:22-26; John 12:12-13; James 1:2-8

Forgiving: Mark 11:25-26; Luke 17:1-4; Ephesians 4:25-32

Birth and Resurrection of Christ: Luke 2:1-20; 24

New Birth: John 3:1-21; Romans 10:1-17

Good Shepherd: John 10:1-15, 22-30

Death/Resurrection of Lazarus: John 11:1-44

Peace: John 14

Abiding in Christ: John 15:1-17
Holy Spirit: Acts 1:4-8; 2:1-13
Justified by faith: Romans 4
Christ's Love: Romans 5
Free from sin: Romans 8
Spiritual gifts: Romans 12
Freedom in Christ: Romans 14
Gifts and diversities: 1 Corinthians 12
Love: 1 Corinthians 13
Walking in the Spirit: Galatians 5:16-26
Love, light, and wisdom: Galatians 5:1-21
Armor of God: Ephesians 6:1-20
Humility: Philippians 2:1-24
Right thinking: Philippians 4
Youth in ministry: 1 Timothy 4
Be strong: 2 Timothy 2
Faith: Hebrews 11
Patience in trials: James 1
The tongue: James 3:1-12
New Heaven, Earth, Jerusalem: Revelations 21

Acknowledgments

Rev. Ron Masters, my husband, for his love and support.

Karen Westerfield and JoAnn Ellis, my daughters, for their prayers and reinforcement.

Rev. Norman and Nathan Tosten, my brothers, for believing in me.

Jeanette Green, my sister, for simplifying M & M.

The late Rev. Wayne and Carol Masters for praying.

Lucy Corbin for taking time to critique this manuscript.

Evelyn Thorness for her special advice and for the quotes of her husband, the late Rev. Birger M. Thorness.

My friends for their prayers and encouragement.

Donna Woge for idea of M & M for Kids.

Holly Burtt for her research in child care.

The men and women who attended seminars and helped shape Memorize and Meditate.

Kin Millen for putting me in touch with right people.

Carolyn Haynes for her insight and intuition.

The late Dr. Ronald Haynes, Thomas Nelson Publishers senior acquisitions editor, for his work and creativity.

Other books by LaVonne Masters

Some through the flood

The Bible Verse Book

Memorize and Meditate

More than Survival:
Complete Communication with God

Bonus Content
More than Survival:
Complete Communication with God

Chapter 1
Communication with God

Victoria, Elizabeth and I followed the people in the tour groups and took off our shoes and carefully placed them alongside all the hundreds of other shoes outside the Wat Phra Keo—the royal temple of the Emerald Buddha, one of the most venerated sites in Bangkok, Thailand. My husband and I were taking care of our granddaughters for several weeks as our daughter JoAnn and her husband Reid finished their classes for their Master's degree in international education.

To entertain the girls, I decided to take a few tours with them. We toured palaces and many other tourist sites. This particular tour included the Emerald Buddha—a carved image made of solid green jade and gold.

Now as we gingerly continued barefooted into the temple, Victoria, 9, and Elizabeth, 7, held onto each of my hands. I had some reservations about taking my granddaughters into a place where the belief system totally differed from ours, but I thought it may be a teaching opportunity.

As we entered, there were about a hundred people crowded near the front bowing on their knees, and some even prostrating themselves as they brought their petitions to the Emerald Buddha. Many of them prayed aloud.

It struck me as futility for all these intelligent-appearing people from all over the world trying to communicate with an image who did not hear them, see them, or talk to them.

I said quietly to my granddaughters, "To think, this god can't see, hear or talk."

Victoria added, "And he can't even grant their requests."

I realized she assessed the situation correctly and quickly. I had no need to fear the girls would think this was the Almighty God or a representative of His. Victoria saw immediately that there was no communication or interaction with this image.

People around the world possess this deep need to fellowship and commune with the living God. Faithfully they will pray and offer sacrifices to gods or images. Often, because of false gods inability to communicate, there may be misconceptions about the ability of the true God to communicate. Many consider this impossible.

Fellowship and complete communication with the living God are possible. It is not mystical to commune with God. It is not difficult or time-consuming. It involves just five key features:

Choosing God, taking time with Him
Loving God, getting to know who He is
Conversing with God, listening and talking to Him
Asking of God, learning how to ask Him
Winning with God, taking action for Him

Communication with God plan is practical and easy. Anyone can do it because God meets us where we are as we are. God shows no favoritism. We don't have to exhibit a certain I.Q., belong to the preferred crowd, or grow up in the "right" culture. We don't have to assume a "religious" tone of voice, speak with pious-sounding words, or attain a certain spiritual level. The Bible says: "Draw near to God and He will draw near to you."

"You" includes everyone—you and me. He desires closeness with all of us. He's waiting to come to us with love and understanding.

Yet, He doesn't force us into nearness with Him. We're not marionettes. We have a choice—to choose fellowship with Him.

The Bible tells us about the importance of fellowship with God. God created us for this purpose. We are all searching for this kind of relationship. When we're not in Communication with God, we're not fulfilled. William Morris expressed this thought well when he said: "Fellowship is Heaven, and lack of fellowship is Hell; fellowship is life, and lack of fellowship is death."

With fellowship and intimacy, we thrive. Intimacy with God satisfies.

J. B. Phillips said, "God is the great reality." Fellowship with God, then, can be the greatest reality experience of our lives. This reality of Communication with God gives us ability to more than survive.

God's primary plan for spiritual development is for us to communicate with Him, and good communication is a growing process and development. Then, best of all, our relationship with God brings benefits—the supplying of our basic needs.

Abraham Maslow developed the hierarchy of human needs. He taught that those needs were necessary in the development of human potential. They are: survival, security, love, self-esteem, self-actualization.

Psalm 34:10 tells us these needs can be a certainty by Communication with God. "But those who seek the Lord shall not lack any good thing."

Seeking God and supplied needs become synonymous. We can't have one without the other.

21093513R00046

Made in the USA
Charleston, SC
06 August 2013